Hip Ho

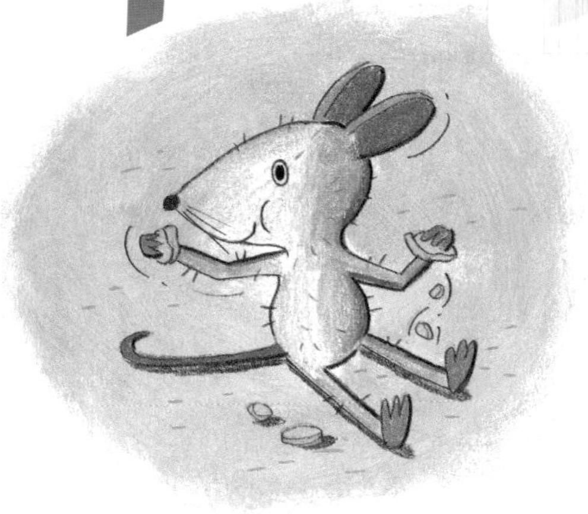

Jane Langford
Illustrated by Christina Bretscheider

RIGBY

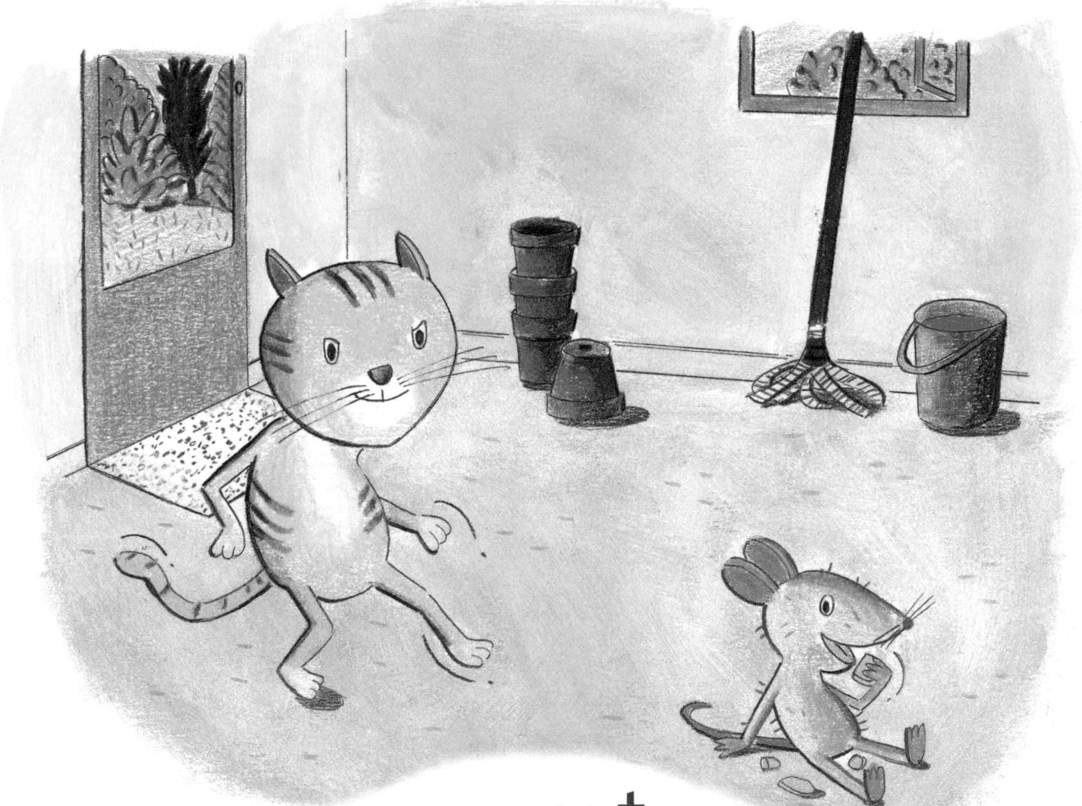

a cat

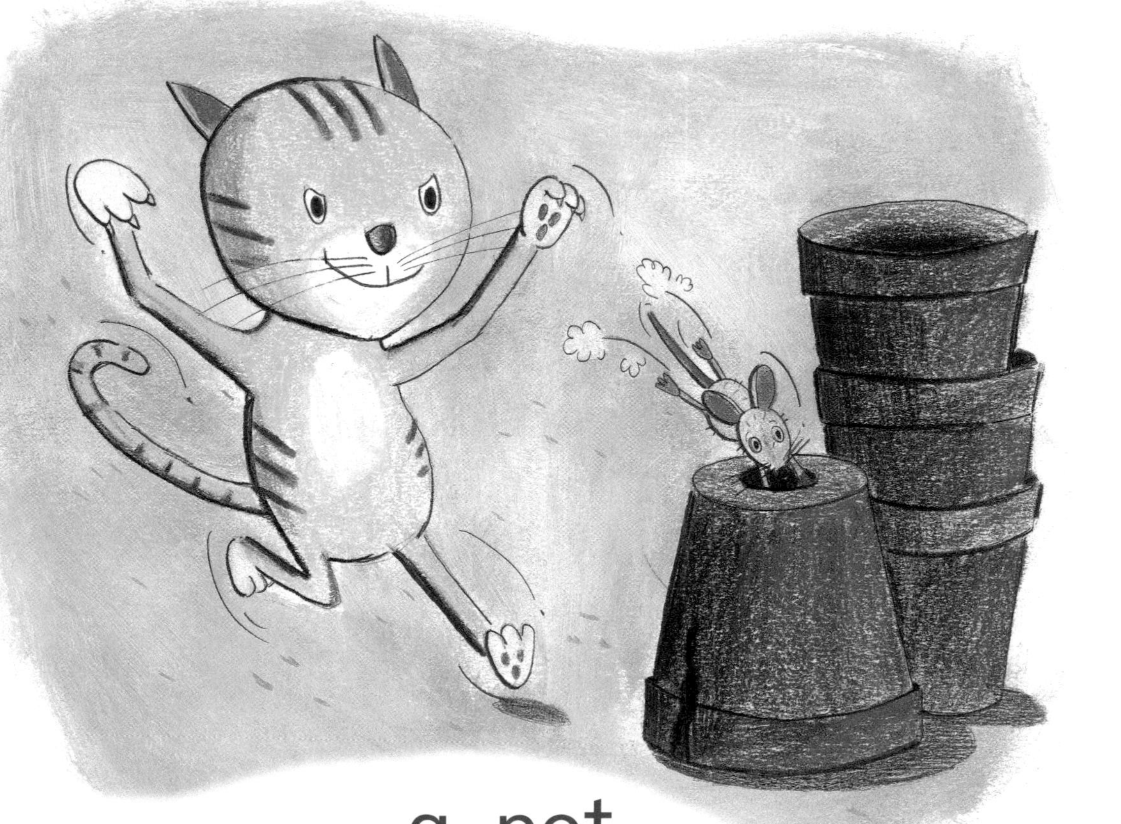

a pot

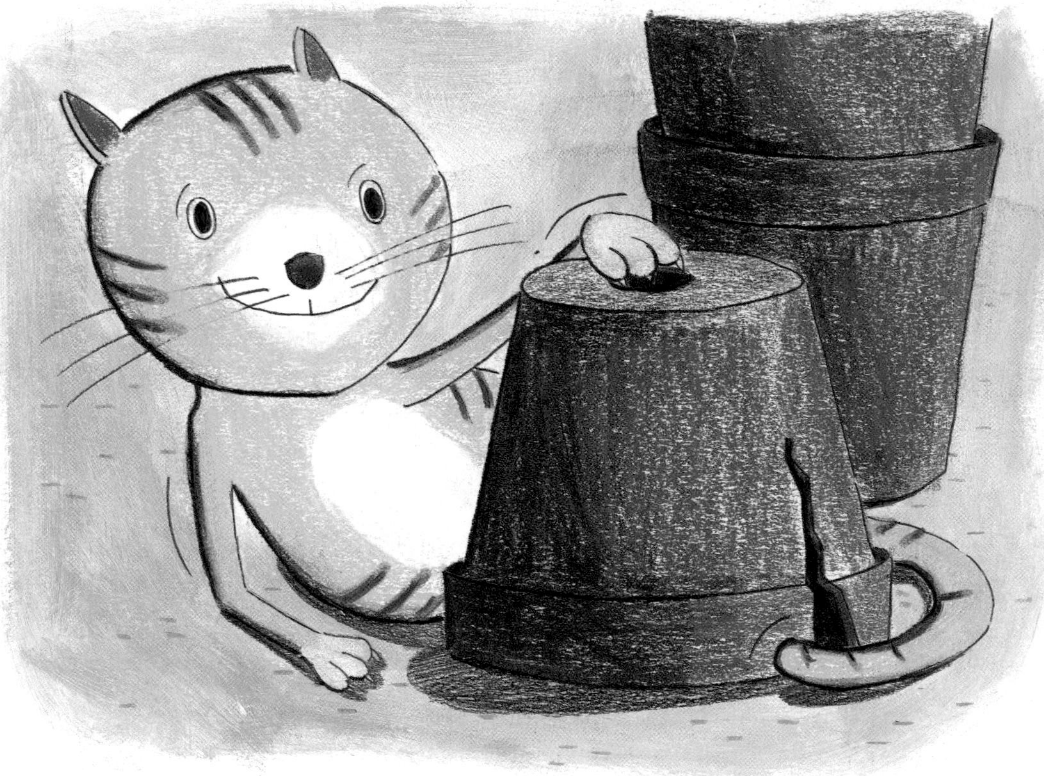

a pat and a tap

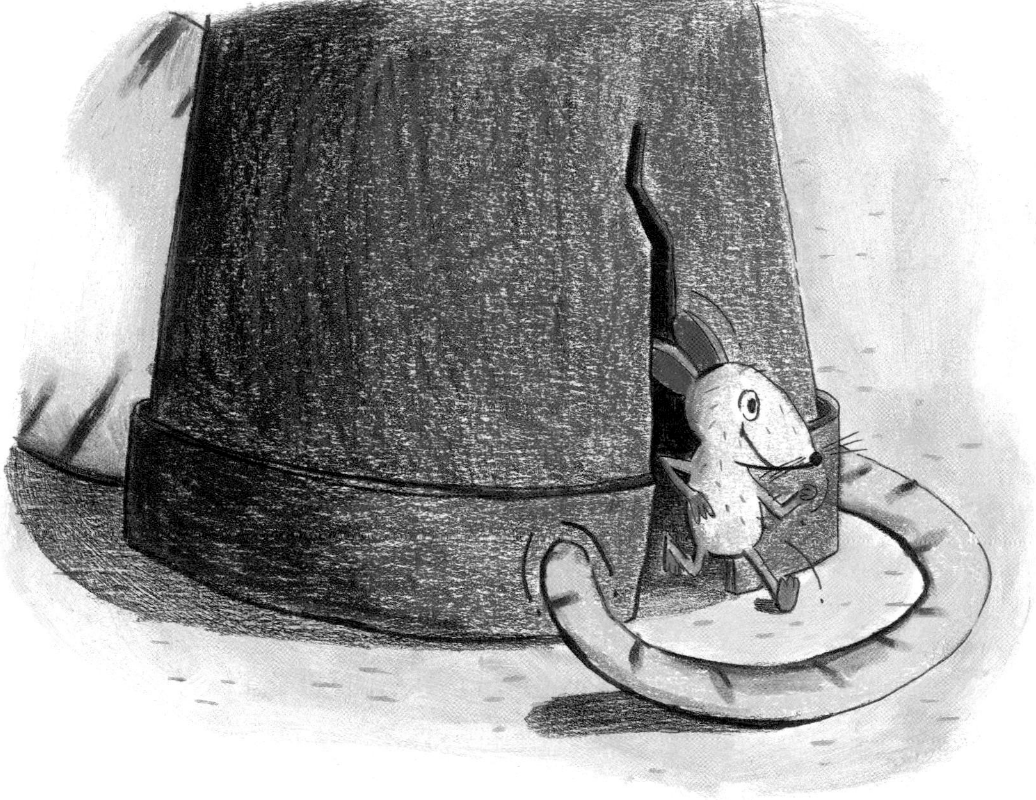

a gap

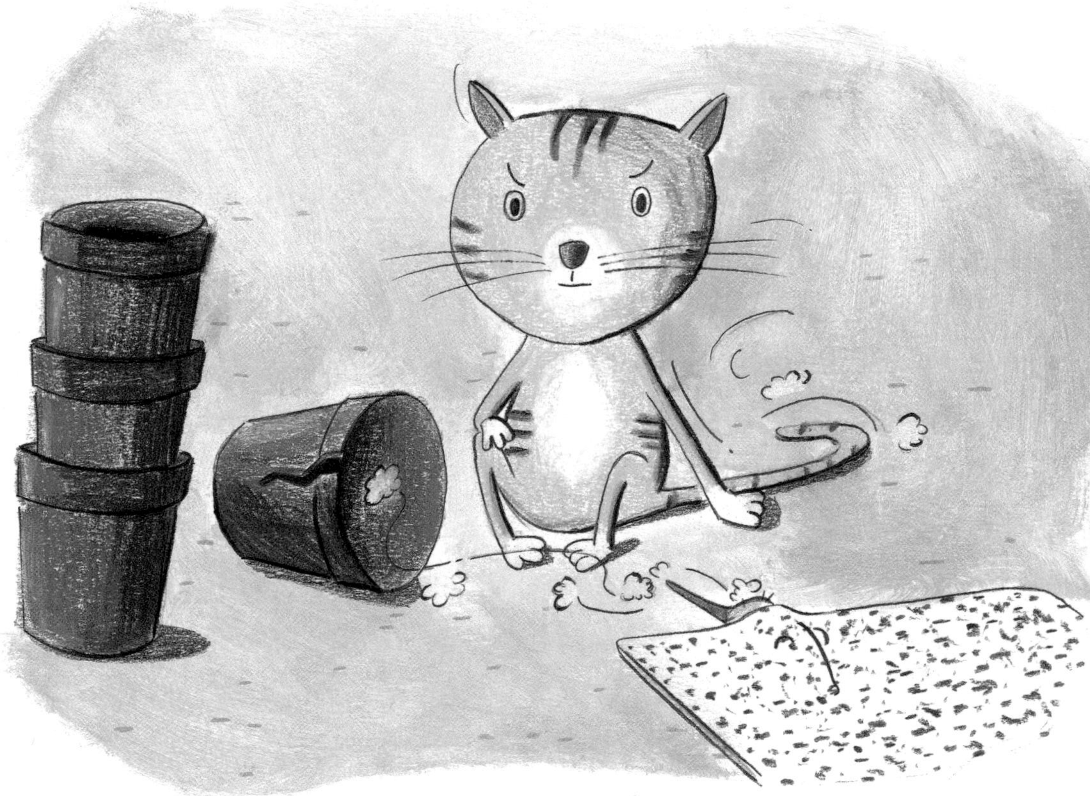

a mat

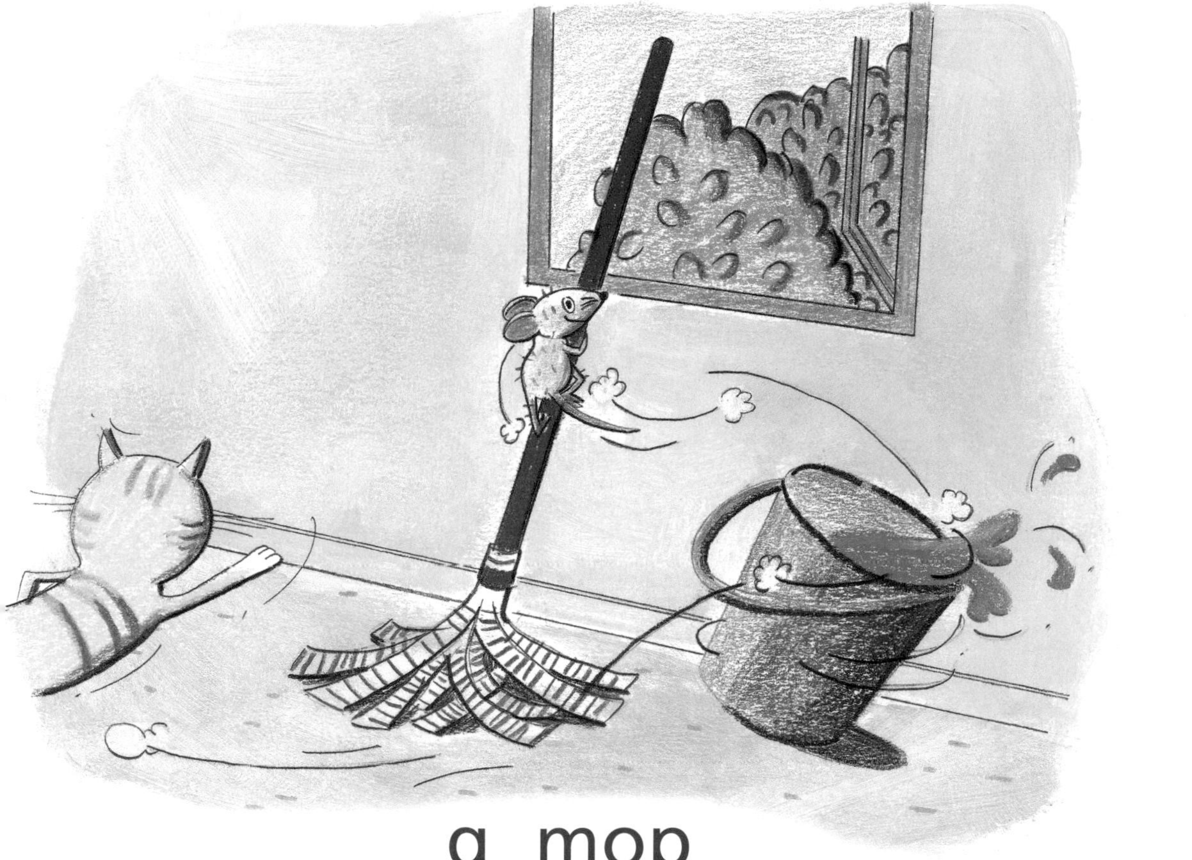

a mop

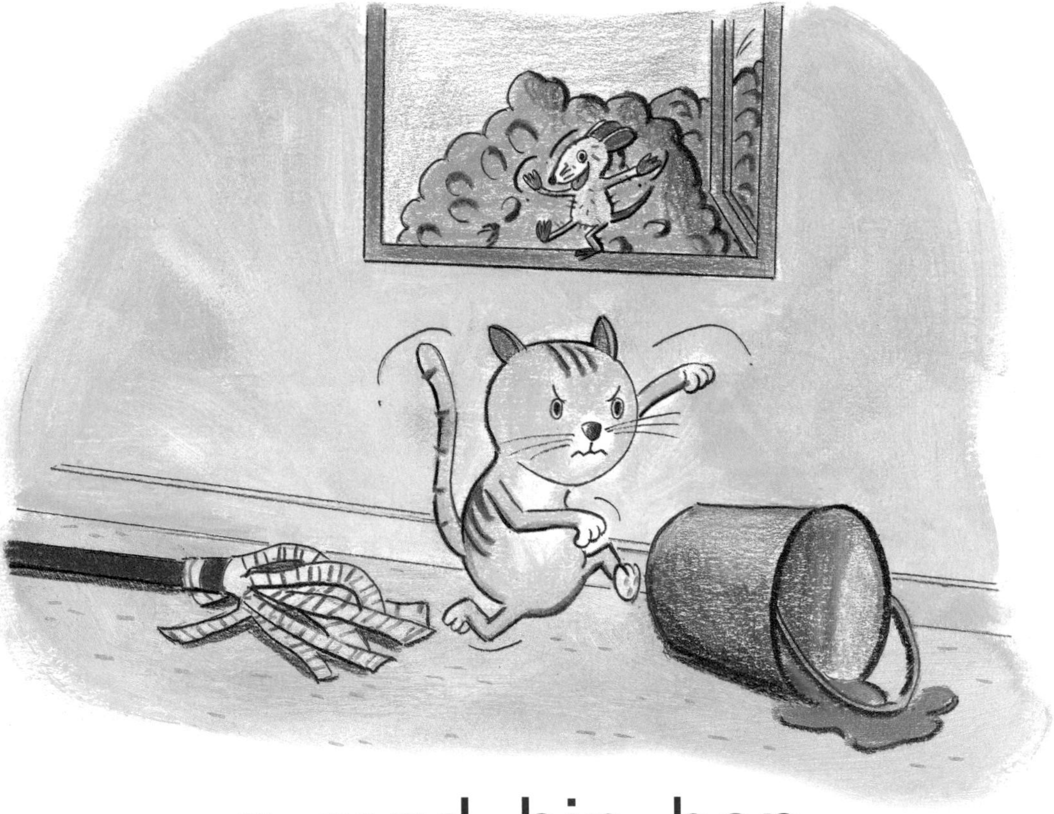

a mad hip hop